Foster Youth Share Their Ideas for Change

Number 3 in a series of youth work resources

Foreword by
Hillary Rodham Clinton

Janet Knipe & Joy Warren

CWLA Press • Washington, DC

California Youth Connection • San Francisco, CA

CWLA Press is an imprint of the Child Welfare League of America. The Child Welfare League of America (CWLA) is a privately supported, nonprofit, membership-based organization committed to preserving, protecting, and promoting the well-being of all children and their families. Believing that children are our most valuable resource, CWLA, through its membership, advocates for high standards, sound public policies, and quality services for children in need and their families.

© 1999 by Janet Knipe. All rights reserved. Neither this book nor any part may be reproduced or transmitted in any form or by any means, electronic or mechanical, including photocopying, microfilming, and recording, or by any information storage and retrieval system, without permission in writing from the publisher. For information on this or other CWLA publications, contact the CWLA Publications Department at the address below.

CHILD WELFARE LEAGUE OF AMERICA, INC.
440 First Street, NW, Third Floor, Washington, DC 20001-2085
E-mail: books@cwla.org

CURRENT PRINTING (last digit)
10 9 8 7 6 5 4 3 2 1

Cover design by Veronica J. Morrison

Printed in the United States of America

ISBN # 0–87868-748-3

Library of Congress Cataloging-in-Publication Data

Knipe, Janet.
    Foster youth share their ideas for change / by Janet Knipe & Joy Warren.
      p.   cm.
    Includes bibliographical references.
    ISBN 0-87868-748-3
    1. Foster children--California--Attitudes. 2. Foster children--Services for--California. 3. Foster home care--Government policy--California. 4. Foster home care--California--management. 5. Child welfare--Government policy--California.   I. Warren, Joy, 1973-
II. Child Welfare League of America.   III. Title.
HV883.C2K56   1998   98-47359
362.73'3'09794--dc21   CIP

Dedication

This book is dedicated to current and former foster youth throughout California whose thoughtful and articulate ideas are invaluable to all of us.

Contents

Foreword from Hillary Rodham Clinton   vii

Acknowledgments   ix

Introduction   1

Methodology   5

Findings   7

Patterns in the Focus Group Comments   17

Conclusion and Policy Recommendations   19

Report from CYC Conferences   23

About the Authors   47

Foreword

I first had the pleasure of meeting with foster youth members of California Youth Connection in the Spring of 1998. These bright, hope-filled young people touched my heart and brightened my spirits as they spoke of their own experiences in the foster care system. Although they have faced great adversity, they have achieved great personal triumphs. It is most impressive that these young people have chosen to devote their time and energy to bettering foster care for other children. California Youth Connection (CYC) is a unique advocacy group composed entirely of current or former foster youth who work to improve foster care and to protect the rights or foster children. CYC members go both to the community and the state capitol to promote youth participation in policymaking and legislative change. These young people share with us a powerful wisdom and fresh insights into what does and does not work in child welfare.

There are priceless lessons to be learned from these young people. Social workers, administrators, legislators, and advocates can be enlightened and edified by the thoughtful ideas they present. It is my hope that the work of CYC will serve as an example for communities across the country so that they will offer to young people who are aging out of foster care the support and assistance they need to become healthy, successful adults. We must all work together to ensure that the end of foster care does not mean the end of caring for these special young people. As you read these pages, I hope that you will feel the same sense of inspiration that I felt when I first met them.

Hillary Rodham Clinton

Acknowledgments

I would like to thank Emily Bruce and Myeshia Grice for their assistance in the facilitation of the focus groups and, with Joy Warren, for their expertise in the child welfare field, which greatly contributed to the completion of this final report. I would also like to thank Sheryl Fullerton for her expertise with the overall conceptualization and development of the project and her editorial assistance with the final report.

Janet Knipe

Introduction

As we near the end of the twentieth century, we are questioning all our assumptions about welfare policy. We have passed new laws, adopted new policies, and discontinued old programs. While we debate our responsibilities to struggling families and their children and consider the role of the child welfare system in protecting children and preserving families, we have seldom listened to children and youth.

Policymakers, politicians, judges, social welfare professionals, and researchers have all had input into what should be done, as illustrated by the proliferation of programs ranging from family support to family reunification to adoption. But we have not listened to those who have experienced the foster care system and its programs directly. Foster youth have not been considered reliable stakeholders in the system—but nothing could be further from reality.

Current and former foster youth are essential participants in any reevaluations or changes, because no one can be clearer or more articulate about how the foster care system has—or has not—worked for them. Their voices must be heard, as we revisit our child welfare mission and examine how the constructions of adoption, family preservation, family reunification, emergency response, long-term foster care, and other programs actually play out in the lives of youth and their families. We must discover whether their experiences match our assumptions.

The California Youth Connection (CYC) is a statewide advocacy organization of 250 current and former foster youth. CYC is unique, in that it is run by the youth themselves. By working on legislation and collaborating with their own local county social service departments, these youth are striving to improve policies that affect youth in the foster care system. CYC members identify issues they believe should be addressed, based on their experiences, and work to educate the public and policymakers about their unique needs.

CYC was formed in 1988 in response to the growing concern that the voices of foster youth (the true consumers of child welfare services) were not valued or included in the development of policies that controlled their lives and destinies. Some policymakers are aware of this exclusion, but have made no moves to address it. Furthermore, CYC youth found that many policymakers who were determining the priorities and outcomes of the child welfare system had never spoken with anyone who had actually experienced that system. According to Johnson, Yoken, and Voss, "The children themselves have much to teach us about those aspects of our family foster care system that are working well for them and their families, and those that need modification" [1995, p. 961].

CYC creates a vehicle for youth to study issues, articulate their needs, and develop solutions and policy recommendations. CYC youth agree with Bush and Gordon that

> the participation of children who are affected by child welfare decisions is a necessary ingredient for effective decision making ... there is an untapped potential for improving social services and contributing to family stability by seeking out and paying attention to their

views. These views are important because children are the *best source* [italics added] of information on some outcome measures. [Bush & Gordon 1982, p. 309]

Although CYC members have regularly discussed ways to improve the foster care system, they had not been asked directly how the child welfare system has worked for them and their families. In an effort to assess the current child welfare system from the youth's perspectives, CYC decided to talk to foster youth from across the state and then evaluate how their experiences matched current assumptions and knowledge. Rather than using a survey questionnaire or other interview methods, the organization decided to use focus groups, which provide a more comfortable peer group setting that is less intimidating and that encourages foster youth to share their experiences more openly and to exchange ideas in a more analytical and thoughtful way. Focus groups also have the advantage of gathering large amounts of information from a broad sample relatively quickly.

This paper is a report on those focus groups. Its intent is to accurately depict the ideas, concerns, and recommendations of the youth who participated and to educate those who create legislation, make child welfare policy decisions, adjudicate foster and adoption cases, or in any way work with or affect these young people's lives.

Notes

Bush, M., & Gordon, A. C. (1982, July). The case for involving children in child welfare decisions. *Social Work Journal*, 309-314.

Johnson, P. R., Yoken, C., & Voss, R. (1995, Sept/Oct). Family foster care placement: The child's perspective. *Child Welfare*, 74, 959-974.

Methodology

CYC has five geographic regions and 20 chapters throughout the state. To ensure the greatest representation of views and participation, focus groups were conducted in each of the five regions, plus two additional groups—one in the Southern region and one in the Central Valley region. Since more than 40% of California's foster youth live in Los Angeles County, and because of the large geographical distances from the northern to the southern ends of the Central Valley, these two groups were added to ensure appropriate representation. Focus groups were scheduled in San Francisco, Sacramento, Redding, Visalia, San Diego, and Los Angeles, but youth from all participating chapters in the surrounding regions were invited to attend.

Participation in the focus groups was voluntary, sometimes taking place at a regular CYC meeting, and other times at a meeting set up solely for this purpose. Approximately 55 youth, ages 16 to 20 (roughly one-fifth of CYC's membership statewide), participated in the seven focus groups. Some 60% of the youth were still in foster care; most of the remaining 40% had emancipated within the last two years. Adult supporters from the chapters also attended the sessions, but did not participate. The groups were facilitated by Janet Knipe, CYC Statewide Coordination; Myeshia Grice, CYC Youth Organization; and

Emily Bruce, doctoral student at the School of Social Welfare, University of California at Berkeley.

The focus groups addressed the central overarching question: What were your experiences as young people in the child welfare system? To focus the discussions further, facilitators asked the participants to concentrate on seven key programs or processes in child welfare:

- emergency response
- court process
- family reunification
- long-term foster care
- family support
- family preservation
- adoption

To be sure that the youth all had the same concept of each of the programs, facilitators led discussions to help youth define and clarify their understanding of each one. Each program was then defined in a standardized way across all focus groups. Each group was asked the same questions about each of the programs they had experienced. If participants had not directly experienced newer programs, such as family support or family preservation, facilitators asked them to consider how these programs would have worked for them and their families. This was an especially helpful approach when the discussion turned to adoption, which had not been considered for most of these youth.

Findings

The following findings for each of the seven child welfare programs provide us with invaluable information and key insights, as we reap the benefit of the expertise of the *consumer* of our foster care services.

Emergency Response Program

Of all the topics discussed in the focus groups, the concerns about emergency response processes and procedures were the most striking. Since all youth had entered foster care through this program, they had firsthand knowledge to draw on. More than anything else, the youth objected to the lack of information they were given about what was going on, why they were being removed, and what was going to happen to them (and to their parents and siblings). There was near unanimity that social workers "talked down to them" or "talked to [them] in a childish way and were not forthcoming with clear information." When youth asked social workers what was going on, they were told, "We can't tell you." One youth said, "They kept telling me, you're going home, you're going home. Here it is eight years later and I'm still not home." Another youth suggested that, instead of abruptly removing children from school, the social worker should meet with the whole family and explain to everyone what was going to happen.

Youth agreed that there should be more surprise visits to the home, but did not agree on visits to schools. Some wanted school visits, others did not. Those who wanted school visits thought these visits would allow children to speak more openly about their family situations; others were opposed to school visits because of the loss of privacy and the stigma that would be attached to them if their friends saw them interviewed by a social worker or police officer. They all believed, however, that the social worker should always interview the child alone, even if a parent were nearby, because the child should have the opportunity to express his or her feelings about the family more freely. Youth said they would be inhibited if a parent were present.

Youth also stated that police, as well as social workers, could be more sensitive to their needs and more supportive of them during the confusing time when they were being removed from their families. The prevailing desire was to be told the truth, and the consensus was that withholding information was more damaging than anything.

Youth also suggested more training for social workers and police on assessment techniques, since many youth lied to social workers to protect their family, even though they knew they should have been removed. Without exception, the youth felt they should never be escorted from school or their home in a police car; it's not only embarrassing, but also adds to the negative self-image many have as they blame themselves for their family's problems. One youth felt that the removal process she went through was more positive, because the social worker consulted her about a placement with a particular foster family, and this smoothed the transition.

Court Process

The overwhelming view of the youth in these focus groups was that they felt left out of the court process, that their opinions were not taken

Findings

seriously, that their attorney did not represent their interest in court, and that many never actually spoke to their attorney. They voiced concerns about the lack of information about every aspect of the court process: that they had an attorney who should be representing their interests, that they had the right to attend court hearings, and that they could state their preferences in court. Comments such as, "No one asked me, they just told me what would happen," and "The social worker talked to everyone except me," embody the frustration the youth felt about the mysterious court process that seemed, in most cases, to go on without their knowledge. Some youth expressed concerns that they had not been prepared about what to expect. They described long waits for their time in court and feelings of being intimidated once they were in the courtroom. One youth told of the awkwardness of encountering a parent whom she had not seem in some time.

Youth felt that no one involved in the court process had made much of an effort to account for and anticipate the way youth were likely to perceive the court process. These experiences left youth afraid of the court process, uncertain of what the outcome might be, and concerned about how it would change their lives. Even those youth who were included in the court process expressed concerns regarding a lack of preparation about what to expect.

Some youth in the focus groups did report that they had been given more information about court, which gave them the opportunity to choose whether to participate or not. This knowledge gave them a sense of control over their lives that others, who were left out of the process, did not feel. In those instances, a responsive attorney or a judge who sought out the opinions of youth made a great difference in the experience. One youth had court representation who, because he paid particular attention to her case, was able to act as a strong advocate for her wishes.

For the most part, the court process was a mystery to youth participating in the focus groups. In most cases, even if they knew about court or knew that they had an attorney, the youth did not feel their opinion was valued or needed. They expressed anger at being left out of such a critical phase of the child welfare system: the phase that ultimately determines their fate.

Family Reunification

Everyone participating in the focus groups had experienced the family reunification program, although many did not realize that their parents had had a certain amount of time to comply with a reunification plan so that they could be reunited with their children. Several youth stated, again, that the program was not explained to them and that they didn't feel supported in the process. Once the facilitator explained to them that, by law, their parents did have a specific amount of time (12 to 18 months), the groups were generally split on whether that was too little or too much time for the reunification process.

Several youth stated that they thought the Department of Social Services (DSS) had attempted to reunify their families, even though their home situation was quite poor; they would have liked DSS to pay more attention to how their parents were actually behaving. As one youth said, "Don't make the children go home if they don't feel safe." Others felt there was a strong push to reunify with a parent, even though the youth did not have a relationship with that person. As one stated, "I'd rather stay in a foster home than be reunited with someone I never knew, just because he's my biological father." Youth suggested that they should have been consulted more about the process and about visits with their biological parents as a part of their reunification plan. They recommended that they should be asked their preferences as early as age 10.

Those youth who were given information by the social worker on family reunification and who understood the program reported more positive feelings about it. They supported reunification, because they wanted their parents to be given a chance. At least one youth stated that she thought reunification services should be extended past 18 months, because "we should always be trying to get back together." Knowing that their parents had this time gave youth a more realistic sense of their parents' abilities or limitations, and, if reunification did not work and they moved into long-term foster care, the youth tended to blame themselves less for their parents' problems and their removal. As one youth said, "At least the kid knows they tried; no matter how hard I try, I now know it's never going to be there [family reunified]."

All youth agreed on the need for accurate information about the family reunification program and inclusion of youth in the decision-making process. While some believed that 18 months was too short, and some too long, they did concur that there should be a relationship between the child and parent for reunification to work. The youth believe that, in some cases, social workers had pursued reunification based more on the biological ties than on any emotional relationship and sense of attachment. They emphasized the importance of their input in the process; they believe they know better than anyone else how visits with their parents have gone and whether they feel safe being at home.

Long-Term Foster Care

Although many of the youth in the focus groups believed that foster care had made them stronger, had been better for them than their family situations, and was clearly "necessary," they also felt that there were many policies that did not meet their needs as "consumers of the system." They felt that recruitment and screening of caretakers needed to be improved, as well as training, especially on communication and confidentiality. Many cited instances when they felt confidentiality was breached, either with a therapist or another caretaker, when they complained about their situation or placement.

When this information got back to the caretaker, it jeopardized their relationship because the youth always felt only conditional acceptance from the caretaker. Youth in these focus groups universally agreed that foster home placements were preferable to group homes, because of the possibility of a more family-like setting. They also emphasized that foster care "needs to be significantly better than my experiences at home; in some cases, it's not."

Family Support

Although the family support model is so new to California that none of these youth had experienced it directly, they were asked to imagine how these types of services would have affected their families. When they thought about the prevailing premise that the success of this program depends on the background of the family and its particular dynamics, the youth were generally divided on its possible effectiveness.

Supporters of the concept stressed that the services could help a family solve their problems before they became severe, and that this was preferable and possibly more effective than waiting until their family was in crisis. They believed that a family should have the opportunity to receive counseling early on and that, with support from a strong extended family, this program could have avoided an escala-

Findings

tion of problems that would send a child into foster care, especially if the family could be realistic about the abilities to overcome their problems.

Many youth agreed that it would be good for the family to be eligible for support funds during a financial crisis to pay bills temporarily or make a deposit for housing, thereby averting the need to remove children into foster care. But they also saw the need to protect against the possible misuse of these funds and suggested that social workers make the payments themselves, or require receipts from the family for any expenditures.

Youth who were skeptical of family support services stressed the fragility of their family system and said they believed that bringing in counselors or other community/family members into the problem-solving process would be a breach of privacy that their families would not tolerate. Some stated that they had lived in so many places that they had no community support and that their family often remained isolated from others who could help. Many raised concerns about any money going to the family for the payment of bills. They felt strongly that if the money were given to their family directly, with no strings attached, it might well support the destructive behavior already established in the family system.

Across all focus groups, youth were generally evenly split on the issue of family support programs, with some who believed it is better to try anything to avoid foster care and others who felt their family was too tenuous and lacked the community/extended family support to make this model successful. As one youth said, "My extended family just sat by and watched everything happen and didn't reach out to help. No program could have made them care."

Family Preservation

About 25% of all focus group participants had actually experienced some type of family preservation services. However, almost all the youth felt that by the time these services would be applied, their families' problems would be (or were) entrenched and that their parents would lie or misrepresent the situation to the social worker or counselor who came in to work with the family. Conceding that all families are different and that these services could work if their parents "had an open mind," the majority of youth said that a counselor coming into the home would not be welcome. As one youth stated, "My mother would say 'No stranger comes into my house and tells me how to raise my kids. I brought you into this world. I know how to raise you.'"

Many youth stated that their parents would "pretend," "lie," and "not act normal" until the counselor left, and then take it out on them. The youth also felt that children would actually be in a more vulnerable position, because they would be blamed by their parents for the family's problems. They worried that if they did or said the wrong thing, they would be taken away, or worse, separated from their siblings.

A small minority of youth favored family preservation, because there would be somebody in the house watching how the family interacted. "It would be better than foster care. I wish I'd had it," said one youth. But the greater number of youth felt strongly that family preservation, especially having a counselor spend a certain amount of time actually in the home, would be ineffective and could, in some instances, make the children more vulnerable.

Adoption

As stated previously, although many young people did not have the option of adoption presented to them, they still had opinions about it.

Clearly, some youth would have liked the option. As one said, "I wished there was someone there for me." To support adoption, however, they wanted to be able to maintain contact with their birth families, and they stressed that they had been fearful of adoption because they thought they would lose that contact. When the concept of open adoption was explained to them, they felt relieved that they would not have to choose between one family and another and that there would be greater continuity in their lives.

The youth also stressed unilaterally that they never wanted to be separated from their siblings, not only in the adoption process, but also in all other forms of placement. They held this belief even if their biological mother would have had another baby with a different father after they were in foster care. It was "still your family," many youth said, again highlighting their concerns about closed adoptions. Also, youth felt strongly that they should be a part of the decision-making process regarding their own adoption and that an adoption should occur only if they agreed to it.

Many youth talked about being misled about adoption or being told that, by a certain age, they were unadoptable. As one youth said, "I heard rumors through the foster care system that I was too old, but they got my hopes up, and then my mom wouldn't relinquish her rights." This mirrored another comment by a young woman who said, "They should make sure the parents will give up their rights before they ever talk to a child about adoption."

The youth also disagreed with the notion that they were only adoptable at a certain age. As one said, "If I want to be adopted, it should be available to me at any age." At least some youth believed that DSS should not automatically trust all adoptive parents, and that "someone should keep checking" to make sure the adoptive home is meeting the needs of the child. They also raised concerns about a change of status between being a foster child and an adopted child, especially with regard to a loss of assistance with financial aid for college. Finally, young people in all focus groups stressed that adoption should not be considered for everyone, because many feel such strong ties with their biological family and do not want to have to choose one family over another.

Patterns in the Focus Group Comments

Several patterns in the youth comments reflect overall concerns about their experience and treatment in the child welfare system:

- Youth are not given information and are, in fact, treated as objects to be moved from one place to another, rather than as human beings who want to know what is happening to them and those they love. They reported that information which would have helped them through difficult times was withheld under the guise of protection. Youth frequently cited examples of not being told clearly what was happening to them, the parameters of the program they were in, or about the court process.

- Youth's opinions are not solicited by adults in the system; when voiced, their opinions are often disregarded or discounted. They reported being lied to or misled and of being talked down to. Few adults sought out the youth's view as they went about making decisions about their lives and their families. As one youth said, "After all that has happened to us, what you have to say to me is nothing. I can handle it."

- Youth are left with feelings that they have no control over their lives.

- Families and their children often experience a sense of isolation from their extended family and/or community. This isolation raises questions for the youth about the effectiveness of some programs that require the family to interact with outsiders.
- Intervention should occur before there is a crisis, so that a troubled family can accept help long before it is necessary for children to be placed in foster care.
- More continuity is needed in relationships between youth, their families, and social workers.

Conclusion and Policy Recommendations

Child welfare professionals have historically presumed that children should never be consulted about their placement, because they will only complain about it. Another line of thought suggests that, since youth don't understand the complexities of the foster care system, they can't make objective decisions about it. That system itself (including social workers, attorneys, judges, and police) has, however, actually diminished youth's ability to make informed decisions by withholding critical information from them, instead of treating them as valued members of the decision-making team.

In addition, child welfare professionals tend to make judgments about children's ability to participate in decisions about their fate, based on a flawed sense of what is developmentally appropriate. Since many youth have often assumed a parental role in their families, they are generally more mature than others of the same age who come from more stable families. Assumptions about what children can handle are drawn from ways of life that may have nothing to do with what the child has experienced. For that reason, youth in (or about to enter) the foster care system are able to understand and accept what social workers and others may be fearful of telling them.

From youth's comments in the focus groups, it's clear that they are all too aware not only of the troubles within their families, but also of possible consequences. They can therefore be the social worker's best source of information and can be helpful in assessing difficult situations, especially what makes them feel safe or unsafe. It is only right, given these considerations, that they be consulted about their families and their fates.

This point also supports the belief that it is time that we in the child welfare system moved away from a deficit model of looking at families toward a strengths-based approach which incorporates the expertise of the youth themselves as an added resource. Such an approach is consistent with other models around the country that build on youth's strengths. Instead of looking for only what is wrong with a family, let us use the young people to help us identify the strengths that exist and build on them.

Another assumption the youth challenged in these focus groups was the belief that all children wish they had been adopted and that all wish they had never been placed in foster care. Instead, it appears that the youth have a variety of views on adoption; it is not a universally desired outcome for a number of reasons—one of which is the strength of ties to their birth families, dysfunctional as those families may seem to outsiders. They also believed in most cases that foster care was necessary, but that it needed to be better than the situation they were removed from. In many cases, they felt it was not. This reinforces the previous point that these youth have a clear grasp of reality and should be treated as though they do.

There are a number of policy recommendations we can draw from this report on the CYC focus groups:

- Improve communication and information sharing with children and youth at all stages of child welfare programming. Be honest and learn to deliver information to children in developmentally appropriate ways, accounting for advanced levels of maturity among children who have taken on responsibilities beyond their years in the family.

- Include children and youth in the decisions about their future.
- Promote early intervention into family difficulties through such programs as family support *before* there is a crisis.
- Promote better training on communication for social workers, administrators, caretakers, judges, attorneys, and police, emphasizing sensitivity to and inclusion of youth's views.
- Never remove youth from a family or school in a police car.
- Assist social workers in establishing long-term relationships with youth through reduced caseloads and services that promote following a child through all child welfare programs.
- Always include children and youth in the decision about adoption. All siblings should be kept together and adoption should be available to them at any age.

These policy recommendations are attainable and, according to these youth, would vastly improve the foster care experience for them and for those who will be involved in the child welfare system in the future. Through these focus groups, we have a unique opportunity to learn from the "experts," the consumers of our child welfare services, about how these services have impacted their lives. How better to improve policy and practice than to ask these young people to help us? These thoughtful and stimulating remarks can provide all of us with a critical resources as we reshape and rethink our interventions at all points in the child welfare system. How can we best help parents and children in need? Listen to the children.

Appendix A
Report from CYC Conferences

The California Youth Connection (CYC) holds semiannual conferences, at which foster youth present their proposals for reform to a panel of distinguished leaders. Following is a summary of youth's recommendations on topics that were discussed during the 1997 and 1998 conferences. The statements in bold type are youth's specific recommendation; text in italics reflects their feelings about these issues.

Kinship Care

At a time when the number of children living with relative foster care providers is rapidly increasing, these relatives and child welfare officials are calling for less supervision and oversight by child welfare agencies. CYC youth believe that it is best for foster children to stay with family *as long as* the relative can provide a safe and nurturing home.

Safety

- **Do not place children with relatives unless the relative has a criminal record clearance and child abuse background check.** No one should assume that a relative will be a good caretaker simply because he or she is an aunt, uncle, or grandparent. Several youth reported problems in relative placements, including relatives who abused alcohol or drugs, abusive treatment, inadequate food, and rags for clothing while the caretaker's biological children have sufficient clothing.

- **Establish a "trial period" of three months for relative placements.** Conduct drop-in visits, if necessary, and quarterly inspections. Provide youth with access to an ombudsman.

Social Workers

- **Educate social workers on the special needs of children in kinship care.** Social workers should pay special attention to children placed with relatives, because these children may be less likely to report problems in the home, due to loyalty issues. Just as many children feel obligated to protect their parents, they may similarly feel that they have an obligation to protect their grandparents or other relatives.

References

- **Require prospective relative caregivers to submit letters of reference.**

    "You need references to get a job at a fast-food restaurant, but you don't need any references to get a foster child."

Training and Support

- **Provide relatives with training developed specifically for kin providers.** Several of the youth recalled negative experiences that they believe might have been prevented if their relative foster providers had received training.

    "My aunt always used to tell my sisters and me that we were not her kids, and she openly treated our cousins differently. I think it would have been better if she had been trained."

> "I can remember my aunt and my mom fighting for hours. My mom would be on the porch at two in the morning, drunk and screaming that she wanted to see her kids. A foster parent would have called the police, but I think my aunt put up with it because it was her sister. I think someone should have told my aunt that was not appropriate. It was painful for me and my siblings."

- **Establish joint support groups with relative providers and youth in their care.**

Adoption

In California, advocates are teaming up with child welfare agencies to train social workers on the philosophy that permanence is essential to the success of children and that, if children cannot be safely reunited with their parents, then adoption is the preferred option that guarantees permanence.

The Needs of Youth

- **Maintain biological family ties when appropriate.**
- **Consult children about adoption and include them in decisionmaking about their lives.**
- **Make an effort to place children with families with similar cultural backgrounds.**

Sharing Information

- **Encourage open adoptions.**
- **Provide adopted youth with all available information regarding their biological family, including family history and family medical history.** Information helps youth develop a sense of iden-

tity. Also, providing medical history is clearly important for youth's health concerns.

> *"I should be able to tell my doctor if my family has a history of heart disease. I can't do this without information."*

- **Provide adopted youth with the right to review their records when they turn 18.**

Siblings

- **Never separate siblings, unless a child is endangered by keeping siblings together.** Adoption should not take priority over keeping siblings together.

- **Establish a right to visitation for siblings.** If siblings are not adopted together, then it is essential to a child's well-being and sense of identity to maintain sibling relations. CYC youth would like to serve on a task force to address ways to ensure that siblings have the opportunity to maintain relationships after adoption.

- **Give siblings the right to participate in the decision-making process for adoption of another sibling.** This participation should include getting to know the prospective adoptive family and having veto power over the ultimate decision.

- **Train prospective adoptive parents on the importance of maintaining contact between siblings, including visits, phone calls, and exchanging letters and pictures.**

Ensuring Quality Care

- **Keep adoption cases open for 24 months.** Because many youth have lived in poor quality foster homes, they are concerned about the fact that adoptive families are not supervised. Adoption cases should remain open for 24 months as a trial period to determine if the child is safe and satisfied in the adoptive home.

Group Homes

Often, youth are placed in group homes because there are not enough openings in foster homes. Group homes differ from foster homes in many aspects: they use "shift care," which means that staff rotate shifts in caring for the youth in the home, and the structure of many group homes is neither homelike nor family-like. Youth's lives are regulated by a point system where a child must earn points to gain "privileges," such as permission to work and to participate in sports and school activities.

First and foremost, the youth emphasized that no one should be placed in group homes unless one of the following occurs: 1) a youth requests a group home placement, or 2) a youth has *documented* needs that can only be met in a group home. Youth also advocated for meaningful restrictions on placing younger children in group homes. They strongly believe that younger children, particularly those under the age of 13, are likely to perceive such a placement as punishment for something they *"did wrong."*

Otherwise, youth have some basic requests of life in group homes. They want to live in a clean house, to be fed, clothed, and most of all, to feel safe. For CYC youth, a safe group home is one in which there is *"no mental, physical, or sexual abuse and the facility is in good condition."* Overall, they would like to protect against enduring what one youth called, *"The same kinds of verbal and psychological abuse from which the courts just separated them."*

Quality of Life

- **Ensure that youth are placed in the appropriate level of group home care.** Youth are sometimes unnecessarily placed in higher level group homes (including youth who are eligible for foster home placement), reportedly due to a lack of less restrictive placements. Some youth have remained in inappropriate placements for months or even years. Other times, youth have been placed in a group home with other children who clearly had serious needs that were not being met by the group home providers.

- **Restructure the penalties assessed on group home operators who do not maintain sanitary and safe facilities, so that the operators are more strictly held accountable for the condition of their group homes.**

- **Ensure that group homes provide residents with an adequate allowance.** Though regulations require group homes to provide youth with an allowance, many youth are unaware of this right and they do not receive any allowance. Group home children do not benefit from the regulation unless it is enforced.

- **Take an inventory of residents' clothes to ensure that the group home provides adequate clothing.**

- **Require group homes to provide transportation to youth so that they can participate in extracurricular activities, such as after-school sports, clubs, work, and Independent Living Programs.** Though group homes are paid to care for children, many youth reported that their group home providers often claim they are unable to transport youth to activities outside of regular school hours. This excludes youth who are not permitted to use public transportation or who live in areas where public transportation is inadequate from participating in activities that can help to normalize their lives and decrease their feelings of isolation from nonfoster youth.

- **Do not prohibit youth from obtaining outside employment.** This is an urgent matter for older youth who are preparing to live on their own at age 18. If they are not permitted to work, then they are turned out of doors at emancipation and must try to secure themselves a job without having any employment experience or history. Even youth who live in high-level group homes and have behavioral or emotional problems must be permitted to work, because they will one day be required to live independently.
- **Promote more independence in group home youth.** Youth in group homes should be permitted to engage in the activities that help non-group home youth to achieve the developmental milestones that lead them to become more mature and independent young people. These activities include after-school sports, school government, clubs, social activities, employment, taking responsibility for selecting and purchasing personal items, and learning other basic life skills that are learned naturally by youth who do not live in group home facilities.
- **Create a committee of former foster youth to help group home youth with loneliness after they emancipate.**
- **Make group homes more homelike.**
- **Decrease group home placements.** Many youth are placed in group homes when they don't need to be there. More youth should have the opportunity to live in foster homes.

- Make group home outings more family-oriented.
- Create a group home task force in every county and include foster youth representatives.

The Rights of Youth in Group Homes

- Ensure that youth do not suffer retaliation for filing grievances.
- Create an ombudsman office to advocate for youth and to assist them in resolving problems or conflicts in group homes. The ombudsman should be autonomous and independent of any county or the state.
- Post the phone number of the ombudsman in every group home.
- **Clearly post the rules for group homes in every placement, just as the minimum wage laws are posted in every workplace.** Rules should be posted to prevent arbitrary punishment and to ensure that youth are fully informed of the expectations for their behavior.
- Require social workers to keep confidential all information shared by youth.

Education

- Monitor non-public schools for quality of instruction.
- Do not place a child in a non-public school unless there are documented reasons why the child cannot be served in a public school.
- Provide youth in public and non-public schools with tutoring, support, and advocacy.

Appendix A

Delinquent and Dependent Youth

- **Do not place probation youth and dependent youth in the same group homes.** Dependent youth are sometimes placed with probation youth because there are no other placements available. As a result, dependent youth may be subjected to the same restrictions as probation youth, though they have committed no delinquent acts.

Accountability

- **Require group homes to explain how their expenditures maximize services for youth in their care.**

- **Require counties to specify the amount of money that group homes are required to spend on clothing per month.**

- **Require group homes to maintain records of the food they serve and require nutritionists to review food service to ensure that the youth are provided with adequate food.**

Staff

- **Screen group home staff more carefully.** Some youth have lived in group homes where staff were later found to have criminal records, including felony convictions.

- **Establish clear procedures and guidelines for staff dismissal.** Staff are frequently reprimanded for inappropriate actions that youth believe warrant dismissal. With an understanding of the types of staff behavior that will lead to dismissal, a group home could reduce what youth perceive as a lax, arbitrary, non-child-centered operation.

- Include foster youth in the hiring process for prospective staff.
- **Ensure better trained staff.** Use current and former group home youth to train staff.
- Hire racially diverse staff.
- Hire young staff who have personal experience living in group homes.
- **Require all staff to pass drug tests.** Some youth have been exposed to drug use by staff.
- **Require prospective staff to complete standard psychological testing.** Other professions, such as law enforcement, screen prospective hires with psychological tests.
- Staff should treat youth with more respect.
- Staff should be required to have a minimum of a high school diploma and child development training.
- Conduct searches of staff if a youth has reason to believe that a staff member has taken one of the youth's belongings.

Services for Teens

- Create a special category of true emancipation homes that focus on preparing youth for independence, where the youth are actually involved in the operation of the home.
- **Establish guidelines for group homes regarding preparation of youth for emancipation. Require group homes to make independent living training a part of daily life.** Youth should have the same opportunity that youth who live with their biological

Appendix A

parents have in terms of helping to make meals, to iron clothes, and to perform other tasks in preparation for life on their own.

- Allow and encourage the participation of youth in extracurricular activities, such as sports and student government.

Independent Living Program Participation

- **Enforce the requirement that group homes provide access to Independent Living Programs (ILP) to youth.**
- **Do not permit group homes to deny access to ILP as a form of discipline.**
- **Require county ILP staff to visit group homes to ensure that youth are provided with access to ILP.** County ILP staff should report to Community Care Licensing those group homes that do not provide such access.

Community Care Licensing

- **Create confidential customer satisfaction surveys to be conducted by the youth residents of their group homes.** Keep evaluations on file with Community Care Licensing (CCL).
- **Require CCL to visit group homes every three to six months.**
- **Require CCL to interview all residents during every visit to a group home. Ensure that all interviews are private and confidential.** An overwhelming number of youth who have lived in group homes do not recall being interviewed by CCL. One reason is that CCL often visits during school hours, when youth are unavailable for interviews. Also, some youth have reported that group homes will plan outings for the day that CCL conducts a visit.

- **Require CCL to conduct unannounced inspections of group homes.** Although CCL does not notify group homes of the time of their annual visits, group homes often determine the dates of visits in advance. Some providers notify each other when CCL is in the area, while others can roughly determine the date of the visit based on the date of their last inspection.

- **Create "emancipation assistant" positions for former foster youth, who can assist CCL with development and implementation of youth evaluations.** Emancipation assistants would also act as advocates for youth whose rights are restricted or denied in group homes.

Mental Health

- **Ensure that children are assessed and placed according to their mental health needs.**

- **Ensure that children are not unnecessarily required to take psychotropic medications.**

- **Allow physicians to prescribe psychotropic medications only if the following conditions are met:**
  - staff have obtained a second medical opinion,
  - staff ensure the child receives follow-up doctor visits to monitor progress with the medications, and
  - the child is provided with therapy in addition to medication.

Physical Health

- **Ensure that foster children are able to choose a regular doctor.**

- Provide youth with training on hygiene, sexually transmitted diseases, and independent living skills.

- Hold group homes accountable for ensuring that youth receive adequate health care.

- **Ensure that group homes take adequate precautions in preventing the spread of contagious diseases.** Require homes to provide treatment for such illnesses in a timely manner.

Court Process

Many youth spoke of the mystery of the court process. They uniformly expressed the sentiment that court was an adult event. Though important decisions are made about a child's life in the courtroom, court is not a child-centered experience. Rather, the youth talked about the confusing legal terms and references to code sections that make hearings effectively incomprehensible.

Information

- Provide foster youth with an orientation on the court process.

- Create a newsletter that explains the court process to foster youth.

- **Educate youth about the importance of attending their court hearings.** Many youth have not been fully informed of the importance of attending court hearings. Those CYC youth who have later learned about the potentially life-altering decisions that are made in court felt cheated that they were not encouraged to attend their hearings. Others reported that attorneys, providers, and social workers had discouraged the youth from attending, dismissing the proceedings as irrelevant to the child's life.

If youth do not attend court, they do not have an opportunity to listen to the social worker and attorney reports. This is a serious issue, as youth have stated that they attended court and heard social workers and attorneys give inaccurate or patently false information to the court.

- **Mandate that foster youth be notified of court hearings.** Providers receive notices, but youth do not.

- **Require social workers and attorneys to meet with youth before and after court appearances to keep youth informed of impending changes in their situations and to explain any recent court decisions regarding their case.**

- **Require that youth receive reports from the court.** If youth cannot attend the hearings, they should be informed of the outcomes, including the outcomes for siblings who may have been moved to another placement or been placed for adoption.

- **Create a mentoring program in which emancipated foster youth can help guide foster youth through the court process.**

The Needs of Younger Foster Children

Younger children who enter foster care are particularly vulnerable, because they are unable to advocate for themselves. As caseloads increase with the numbers of young children in out-of-home care, more children are put at risk if social workers are less able to provide adequate services. CYC youth would like to see the foster care system develop more targeted services which acknowledge that an infant has developmental needs that are quite different than the needs of an adolescent.

- **Create a program for younger youth with older and emancipated youth as mentors.** Youth would like to give back to the system by volunteering, mentoring younger foster youth, and educating foster parents, social workers, lawyers, and the general public about the needs of foster youth.
- **Teach youth their rights: to be free from abuse, to have adequate clothing, to have an allowance, to contact a social worker, and to participate in extracurricular activities.**
  > *"My group home told me not to call my social worker, to wait until she called me. The group home was later shut down. I wish I would have known my true rights then."*
- **Provide tutoring.**

The Needs of Emancipating Youth

Youth "emancipate" from foster care at the age of 18, when the State of California terminates all financial support, care, and supervision. Without family to fall back on, many emancipated youth become homeless, drop out of college, or return to the abusive and neglectful homes from which they were initially removed. As one youth stated, *"Emancipation is a scary thing."*

Another youth commented on the irony of the way in which we treat prisoners who are leaving prison, compared to how we treat foster youth leaving care, and pointed out, *"Our society provides prisoners with cash when they exit prison to help them begin their lives on the outside. However, we do not provide our own young people with assistance once they turn 18 and are required to exit foster care."*

One young woman stated the crux of the problem for foster youth that differentiates them from other youth who are not in the system when she said, *"Family is family until you die, unless, of course, you are a foster child. Then you are no longer part of the state's 'family' after you turn 18."*

Preparation for Emancipation

- **Mandate that foster care be made available to youth up until the age of 21.** Currently, the state abdicates all responsibility for foster youth once they reach age 18. It is unrealistic to expect youth to establish complete independence at this age. Foster youth have no family on which they can rely for support or guidance, and many struggle in their transition to adulthood.

- **Provide vocational training and internship opportunities.**

- **Establish resource centers for emancipated youth that provide referrals to affordable housing and jobs, access to computers, and opportunities for recognition of achievement.**

- **Expand transitional housing.**

- **Create emancipation teams that consist of emancipated youth and specialized social workers, who work together to prepare youth leaving the system at age 18.**

- **Require that all youth have a copy of their birth certificate and social security card before they emancipate.**

Independent Living Programs

- **Expand the Independent Living Program (ILP) from its current service population of youth ages 16-18 to youth ages 14-21.**

- **Set uniform basic standards for counties to operate ILPs.** The needs of emancipating youth are so great and so pressing that the state should take leadership in requiring counties to provide specific training to youth, which would include such skills as cooking, budgeting, applying to college, and applying for financial aid.

- **Ensure the ILPs include the following:**
  - household duties (cooking, cleaning, laundry)
  - how to deal with peer pressure and self-esteem issues
  - leadership skills
  - personal hygiene
  - job etiquette
  - sex education
  - computer training
  - assistance with college and financial aid applications and researching scholarships
  - preparation for the SAT and college tours
- **Place cash incentives given to youth for attending ILP in the bank.**
- **Before youth exit care at 18, provide them with an "emancipation start-up kit" that could include pots, pans, sheets, and other basic items for setting up their own households.**
- **Train foster care providers on how to help youth transition to adulthood.**
- **Require foster parents and group homes to provide the county child welfare agency with written verification of the steps they have taken to assist emancipating youth in their transition to independence.**

- Require CCL to audit group home providers for provision of emancipation support services to the youth in their care.

Health Care

- **Inform youth of their rights to Medi-Cal before they emancipate.** Aside from basic health needs, youth also often require health insurance, because many employers and schools require shots and physicals.
- **Provide foster youth with Medi-Cal benefits without a share of cost for one year following emancipation.**
- **Make affordable counseling and mental health services available to emancipated youth.**
- **Mandate medical insurance workshops to teach emancipating youth the following skills:**
  - filling out applications,
  - meeting deadlines,
  - understanding their own medical needs, and
  - researching health care providers so that they can locate a doctor who can handle their specific health needs.

Services

- **Develop "After Care" programs for emancipated foster youth. These programs should**
  - be run by emancipated youth;
  - require participants to maintain a 2.0 minimum grade point average;

- include housing for emancipated foster youth who do not have housing during college breaks because of dormitory closures—such a program may establish a camp to house youth during these closures;

- provide additional funding assistance for former foster youth who attend college or vocational training; and

- include day care for the children of young parents so that the youth can complete their goals by attending school or by working.

Housing

- **Establish a rental assistance fund for youth who are leaving foster care.** It is particularly difficult to obtain housing, because most landlords require a large up-front payment for first and last month's rent and a security deposit.

- **Set up trust funds to assist youth who are preparing to emancipate.** These trust funds could be created by setting aside a percentage of the board and care rates received by foster parents and group homes.

- **Assist youth in obtaining furniture and basic necessities for setting up a household.**

- **Provide foster youth with a reference for consideration for subsidized housing.**

Job Placement and Training

- **Ensure that all ILPs include actual hands-on practical training.**

- **Provide job retention services.**

- Assist youth in securing transportation to and from work.
- Provide funding for youth to buy professional clothes to wear to job interviews.
- **Require government agencies and encourage private employers to set aside a certain number of jobs for emancipated foster youth.** In Los Angeles County, the Department of Children & Family Services gives preference to former foster youth in hiring. This county could be used as a model for other government agencies.

Evaluations

- **Create placement evaluations to be completed by youth.** Social workers and foster care providers complete formal evaluations of children when they leave placements, but youth never have an opportunity to evaluate the providers.

Social Worker Services and Accountability

The youth reported a variety of problems they had experienced with social workers: social workers who did not return calls promptly or who did not return calls at all, workers who did not visit regularly or ever, lack of communication with workers, and a high rate of worker turnover. Many youth reported that they did not understand the role of the social worker, and therefore did not know what responsibilities a worker has to a child. The youth also expressed disappointment in the lack of staff accountability.

Information

- **Create an information booklet that clearly explains the foster care system to youth.** This booklet should include the following:

Appendix A

- a description of the duties and responsibilities
- the responsibilities of foster parents and group home providers
- information on the court process
- grievance procedures

- Create a video to explain the foster care system to youth.
- Create a newsletter to update youth on state and county law and policy changes.

Services/Accountability

- **Enforce the requirement for social workers to make face-to-face visits with youth.**
- **Require social workers to inform all youth of any changes or pending changes in placement, including adoption, for any siblings.**
- **Require social workers to conduct unannounced visits.**
- **Require social workers to facilitate contact between siblings who are not placed together.**
- **Require social workers to fully inform youth of their rights to confidentiality.** If youth are not informed of their right to confidentiality regarding their discussions with social workers, then they are less likely to speak to their workers about abuse or neglect within a foster home or group home, because they fear retaliation.
- **Require counties to provide youth with notice two weeks prior to a social worker change.**

- Create a mechanism for holding social workers accountable if they do not promptly return youths' calls.
- Institute a clear grievance procedure for youth to use to report social workers who do not adequately perform their duties.
- **Require the counties to create an evaluation form for youth to assess the performance of their social workers.** Counties should use these evaluations to determine if certain workers require more training, more supervision, or transfer to a department where employees do not directly work with foster youth.

Caseloads

- **Reduce social worker caseloads.** The youth acknowledged that overburdened caseworkers are hard pressed to perform all of the services needed by youth in foster care. They suggested hiring interns and emancipated youth to help with caseload burdens, as well as better enforcement of the law that limits workers to a specific number of cases.

Communication

- Provide youth with a list of phone numbers of people to contact when their workers are unavailable.
- Establish a 24-hour hotline for youth to call.
- **Reduce the number of social workers who are assigned to an individual youth.** Changing social workers is disruptive and presents a variety of problems for youth, who have difficulty establishing trust or even a working relationship with a worker if they are constantly subjected to worker turnover.

- Hold workshops for youth to learn about programs available through the child welfare agency.

About the Authors

Janet Knipe, M.S., is Statewide Coordinator of California Youth Connection (CYC) in San Francisco, a statewide advocacy organization for current and former foster youth with 20 chapters throughout California. In that position, she is responsible for overall management and program development. Prior to that, she was Program Director for the Contra Costa County Independent Living Skills Program. Ms. Knipe received her M.S. in Clinical/Community Psychology from San Jose State University.

Joy Warren, B.A., who grew up in California's foster care system, is a recent graduate of the University of California at Berkeley. Joy has worked actively in behalf of young people in foster care, both with the California Youth Connection and with the Youth Law Center in San Francisco. Ms. Warren is currently pursuing a degree in public interest law at Yale University.

YOUTH WORK RESOURCES
from the
Child Welfare League of America

Interactive Youth Work Practice
by Mark A. Krueger

Through essays, practice examples, and a curriculum outline, *Interactive Youth Work Practice* promotes the theory that youth develop in moments and interactions. These moments and interactions are enhanced when workers have the capacity to guide, teach, learn, and be *with* youth, with sensitivity to their developmental capacities and readiness for growth and the multiple contexts within which interactions take place. Youth work is viewed as a shared journey, workers and youth going through the day, learning and growing together!

To Order: 1998/0-87868-707-6   Stock #7076 $12.95

Write:	CWLA	Call:	800/407-6273
	P.O. Box 2019		301/617-7825
	Annapolis Junction, MD 20701		
E-mail:	cwla@pmds.com	Fax:	301/206-9789

Please specify stock #7076. Bulk discount policy (not for resale): 10-49 copies 10%, 50-99 copies 20%, 100 or more copies 40%. Canadian and foreign orders must be prepaid in U.S. funds. MasterCard/Visa accepted.

YOUTH WORK RESOURCES
from the
Child Welfare League of America

Housing Options for Independent Living Programs
by Mark J. Kroner

Learning independent living skills and having a safe place to practice those skills is crucial to the success of youth leaving the child welfare system. *Housing Options for Independent Living Programs* describes the variety of housing arrangements (such as shared homes, specialized foster homes, and scattered-site apartments that independent living programs may use and offers numerous examples of how these arrangements have helped youth gain their independence.

This book examines issues related to supervision, funding, budgeting, and special populations. Resources and forms that ILPs may adapt for their own use provide additional help in setting up and running such a program.

To Order: 1999/0-87868-752-1   Stock #7521 $14.95

Write:	CWLA P.O. Box 2019 Annapolis Junction, MD 20701	Call:	800/407-6273 301/617-7825
E-mail:	cwla@pmds.com	Fax:	301/206-9789

Please specify stock #7521. Bulk discount policy (not for resale): 10-49 copies 10%, 50-99 copies 20%, 100 or more copies 40%. Canadian and foreign orders must be prepaid in U.S. funds. MasterCard/Visa accepted.

From the
Child Welfare League of America
and the
American Enterprise Institute
for Public Policy Research

*America's Disconnected Youth:
Toward a Preventive Strategy*
Douglas J. Besharov, Editor

America's Disconnected Youth: Toward a Preventive Strategy identifies adolescence as a time of both great opportunity and risk, when young people experience physical change, intellectual growth, self-discovery, and growing independence—but it also notes that some young people have difficulty making the transition from adolescence to productive adulthood. The editor has recruited well-respected authors to examine mentoring and school-to-work programs as important strategies for assisting these youth. The chapters include in-depth descriptions of the factors that have contributed to keeping these young people from productive adult lives.

To Order: 1999/0-87868-756-4   Stock #7564 $28.95

Write:	CWLA	Call:	800/407-6273
	P.O. Box 2019		301/617-7825
	Annapolis Junction, MD 20701		
E-mail:	cwla@pmds.com	Fax:	301/206-9789

Please specify stock #7564. Bulk discount policy (not for resale): 10-49 copies 10%, 50-99 copies 20%, 100 or more copies 40%. Canadian and foreign orders must be prepaid in U.S. funds. MasterCard/Visa accepted.